POSTCARD HISTORY SERIES

Pennsylvania's Historic Bridges

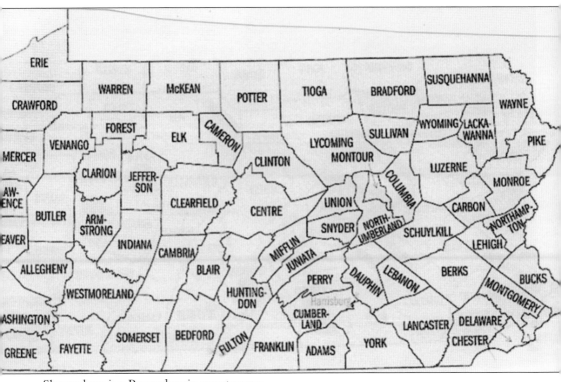

Shown here is a Pennsylvania county map.

POSTCARD HISTORY SERIES

Pennsylvania's Historic Bridges

Fred J. Moll

ARCADIA
PUBLISHING

Published by Arcadia Publishing
Charleston, South Carolina

Printed in the United States of America

Library of Congress Catalog Card Number: 2006939687

For all general information contact Arcadia Publishing at:
Telephone 843-853-2070
Fax 843-853-0044
E-mail sales@arcadiapublishing.com
For customer service and orders:
Toll-Free 1-888-313-2665

Visit us on the Internet at www.arcadiapublishing.com

The Old and New Bridge for Sproul Road, Chester — Swarthmore, Pa.

The construction of bridges has changed significantly over time from the early stone and wooden ones to the current reinforced concrete ones. The different types of bridges have all handled traffic admirably during their course of existence. These two bridges are near Swarthmore in Delaware County. The new reinforced concrete bridge is supporting Baltimore Pike and the old covered bridge in its shadow was on Sproul Road. The covered bridge was referred to as the Sproul Road or the Leiper Quarry covered bridge.

CONTENTS

Acknowledgments   6

Introduction   7

1.   Stone Bridges   9

2.   Uncovered Wooden Bridges   19

3.   Covered Wooden Bridges   25

4.   Suspension Bridges   75

5.   Metal Bridges   83

6.   Concrete Bridges   115

ACKNOWLEDGMENTS

I would like to thank my wife, Shirley, and our three children, Heather, Timothy, and Andrew, for allowing me to devote what I sometimes believe to be too much time to my covered bridge hobby. I remember when the kids were young and I was given the job of babysitting, I would sometimes take the kids to the library or historical society to look through old newspapers from the 1800s to find covered bridge information. The kids would often ask me "are we soon done?" I would promise them a hamburger and fries from their favorite burger place if I could look through just one more newspaper. Many times this promise would be repeated as I picked up "just one more newspaper."

INTRODUCTION

Postcards have often been overlooked as a source of historical information. By looking through old postcards you can learn about the past and follow the growth of America. When you are done looking at the front of the postcard, if it is used, you can turn it over and read the message written on the back. It is here that you will get a sense of what it must have been like living during the time period the postcard was sent. It is also interesting to take notice of the addresses on the early postcards. Usually only a person's name, town, and state were needed. Street numbers, street names, and zip codes were not used, and postage was only 1¢. Postcards have been printed on a wide variety of subjects, including holidays, flowers, animals, art, famous people, buildings, bridges, and so on. Postcards can be divided into different eras. The pioneer era of postcards was before 1898, and the private mailing era was from 1898 to 1901. Postcards produced during these periods were mostly from large cities and were used mainly for advertising by such companies as Kodak, Buster Brown Shoes, and many others. The postcards shown in the pages of this book begin at 1901. The undivided-back postcard era was from 1901 to 1907. These postcards did not have a divided back, and all messages had to be written on the front side of the postcard. The only writing allowed on the back of the postcard was the address. The divided-back postcard era was from 1907 to 1915. Starting with this era, writing was allowed on the back side of the postcard. The left side of the back was for writing a message, and the right side was for the address. The white-border era of postcards was from 1915 to the 1930s. During this era, postcards were printed with a white border around the photograph to cut printing costs. This was done because of the higher costs of postwar publishing. However, most of the postcards produced during this era were not of good quality. The linen era was from the 1930s to the 1940s. During this era, postcards were printed on high–rag content paper that resembled linen. This was an improvement over the white-border postcards. The 1940s saw the start of the chrome era. These were the high-quality color photograph postcards that are still being produced today.

This book takes a look back into time at some of Pennsylvania's early bridges. Some of the types of bridges included in this book are stone bridges, wooden open bridges, wooden covered bridges, iron bridges, concrete bridges, suspension bridges, canal bridges, trolley bridges, railroad bridges, pedestrian bridges, and an aqueduct. Some of the bridges are small footbridges while other bridges are over a mile in length. A majority of the bridges shown on the postcards in this book no longer exist.

Bridges were an important part of our early transportation history. Without bridges, our country would not have progressed and developed as quickly as it did. In Pennsylvania, there has always been an abundance of bridges because of the many streams and waterways that exist, especially in the southern half of the state. During the early years, stone arch bridges and wooden bridges were built, although stone arch bridges are the oldest known bridges in Pennsylvania. Both types of bridges were made from natural material found in the state. The material that was especially in abundance was wood. Pennsylvania was once referred to as Penn's Woods because the state was covered from border to border with tree-covered land. Wood was cheap and could be found near the bridge site. In Pennsylvania in the early 1800s, more bridges were built from wood than any other material. In later years, as Pennsylvania developed and the amount of trees was reduced, logs had to be floated downstream from the northern wooded areas of the state and from New York State. In 1839, iron was introduced as bridge-building material. Railroads were especially interested in using iron for their bridges, which seemed like the next likely step after using wood. But as trains got heavier, there were some bridge failures. When lives were lost, the railroads embarked on a 20-year-long program to replace all their major iron bridges over nonnavigable streams with stone arch bridges. The railroads found that stone arch bridges were more resistant to floods, required less maintenance because they did not have to be sanded or painted, and were able to handle the increasing weight of the newer steam engines. Meanwhile iron continued to be used to build vehicular bridges. In 1855, when the Bessemer converter made steel more economical to produce, steel bridges began to be built. Iron and steel became the most widely used bridge-building materials until concrete was introduced. Reinforced concrete bridges have now become the standard because they require less maintenance and are stronger than previous types of bridges. Even so, there is a lot that can be said for wooden covered bridges. Many covered bridges are still standing across the state even though most are over 100 years old. Pennsylvania once had over 1,526 covered bridges, more than any other state. Currently Pennsylvania has over 200 covered bridges, which is still more than any other state. Over one-quarter of all the covered bridges in the United States are located in Pennsylvania, and each year many tourists come to Pennsylvania to see them. Whatever type of bridge you might be interested in, you will most likely find it in Pennsylvania and in the pages of this book.

One

STONE BRIDGES

LANESBORO, P.A.
One of Nature's
Beauty Spots.

No. 8. STONE BRIDGE AND PUSHERS.   Burton, Pub'r, Lanesboro, Pa.

The Starrucca Viaduct near Lanesboro in Wayne County was built in 1848 by the New York and Erie Railroad. Note the two steam engines on the bridge. The bridge has 18 arches and is 1,200 feet long. Workers were paid $1 a day to build the bridge, and it took one year to complete. The bridge is listed on the National Register of Historic Places, has been designated as a historic civil engineering landmark, and is still being used by the railroad.

This linen-era postcard is of the Washington Inn and stone arch bridge in Valley Forge National Park. The bridge was finished with rubble masonry, or rough stones. The inn was built sometime before 1769. It is said that within the walls of the inn, court-martials were held for George Washington's Continental army during its encampment at Valley Forge during 1776 and 1777.

PICTURESQUE STONE BRIDGE OF FRANKLIN COUNTY, PA.

This is a two-arch stone bridge built in 1851 between Chambersburg and Williamson over Back Creek in Franklin County. Back Creek empties into the Conococheague Creek, which eventually empties into the Potomac River. Because of the high concentration of sandstone, limestone, and other stone deposits in the southeastern half of Pennsylvania, the majority of stone bridges are found to be concentrated in the lower and eastern part of the state.

PICTURESQUE STONE BRIDGE OF FRANKLIN COUNTY, PA.

This is a five-arch stone bridge built about 1830 over the Conococheague Creek between Greencastle and Upton in Franklin County. During construction of a stone bridge, usually a temporary wood frame was built to support the arch stones while the arch was being built. This frame was later removed when the bridge was completed and the mortar was hard. During the early years when Native Americans inhabited this area, Franklin County was originally known as the Conococheague Settlement. The land officially became a county on September 27, 1750.

The Maiden Creek Bridge connected Calcium and Kindt's Corner in Berks County. The bridge was built in 1854 by a Mr. Long and a Mr. Pierce at a cost of $6,609.31. At a length of 311 feet, this was the longest stone arch roadway bridge known to have existed in Berks County. In 1927, the surrounding area, including the bridge, was flooded to create Lake Ontelaunee. However, it is said the top of the bridge can be seen during periods of extreme drought. *Ontelaunee* is a Delaware Indian word meaning "little maiden."

This postcard of the 1798 Witmer's Bridge in Lancaster County illustrates how a stone arch bridge was meant to appear. The half circles formed by the bridge along with the half circles created by their reflection in the water form an almost perfect circle.

The Perkiomen Bridge at Collegeville in Montgomery County is one of the most famous existing stone arch bridges still in use in eastern Pennsylvania. It was built in 1799 at a cost of $60,000. It is said that in 1867, a tollhouse and gate were built to make it a toll bridge, but the local citizens rebelled by burning the tollhouse and throwing the gate into the creek. Over the years, the bridge became so well used and so well known that the lower end of Collegeville around the bridge is referred to as "Perkiomen Bridge."

Point Boulevard with Historic "Stone Bridge" in rear
Johnstown, Pa.

10166

In the background of this postcard a train can be seen crossing the famous Johnstown stone bridge. The bridge is famous but not in a positive way. During the Johnstown Flood of 1889, buildings, all sorts of debris, and people were washed downstream and backed up at the bridge. A whirlpool developed at the base of the bridge, and 80 people were caught in it and lost their lives. In all, over 2,200 people lost their lives in the Johnstown Flood. The stone bridge is still standing.

ASKEW BRIDGE, READING, PA.

The Askew Bridge was built on Sixth Street in Reading in 1857 at a cost of $27,804.85. The bridge carried westbound trains of the Reading Railroad to and from the Reading Outer Station. The stones were laid in an ellipsoidal arc. Each stone had to be cut to the precise prescribed arc. The bridge, listed on the National Register of Historic Places, is still standing and is considered one of the most unusual bridges of its kind in the United States.

This is the Brilliant Cutoff Viaduct over Silver Lake near Pittsburgh. The bridge was named after the nearby Brilliant Oil Refinery. The viaduct was built between 1902 and 1904 by the Pennsylvania Railroad to help trains bypass downtown Pittsburgh. The bridge consists of five stone arches and one steel plate girder span. Over time, Silver Lake was filled in and a drive-in movie theater was built near the base of the bridge. Today industrial buildings occupy the area at the base of the bridge.

PENNA. RAILROAD BRIDGE OVER CONESTOGA RIVER, LANCASTER, PA.

Here is a nighttime scene of a stone arch Pennsylvania Railroad bridge in Lancaster County. Reflections of buildings and a full moon can be seen on the Conestoga River. *Conestoga* is a Native American word meaning "place of the immersed pole." Note the car parked on the left, possibly belonging to young lovers on this moonlit night.

This postcard is of a stone arch railroad bridge in southern Lancaster County. The brick building framed between one of the arches of the bridge is the Lancaster Water Works. Also take notice of the small wooden bridge in the shadow of the large stone bridge.

This photograph, taken in the early 1900s, shows an impressive stone arch railroad bridge located along Wissahickon Drive in Fairmount Park in Philadelphia. It is said that the word *Wissahickon* is a combination of two Lenape Indian words, *Wisaucksickan*, meaning "yellow colored creek," and *Wisamickan*, meaning "catfish creek." The bridge was part of the Philadelphia and Reading Railroad system.

P. & R. R. R. Bridge   Schuylkill River near Tuckerton Pa.

Gustavus A. Nicolls designed and built this Pennsylvania and Reading Railroad bridge over the Schuylkill River during 1855 and 1856, four miles north of Reading at Tuckerton. The bridge is sometimes referred to as "Peacock's Lock Bridge" because of a nearby canal lock by the same name. The bridge has nine stone arches, each with a diameter of 63 feet. The circular openings between the arches are 12 feet in diameter and were designed to reduce the weight of the bridge and to add a unique and decorative appearance to the bridge. The bridge is still standing.

Bridge of Sighs, Pittsburgh, Pa.

The Bridge of Sighs in Pittsburgh was built in 1888 and was once used to transport prisoners from the Allegheny Court House to the Allegheny County Jail. The bridge was named for a similar bridge used for the same purpose in Venice, Italy. It was in this dark and dreary setting of the Allegheny County Jail that the jail scenes from the movie *Silence of the Lambs* were filmed.

64 BIRD'S-EYE VIEW OF ROCKVILLE BRIDGE, LONGEST STONE ARCH BRIDGE IN THE WORLD, HARRISBURG, PA.

This linen-era postcard shows the Rockville Bridge just north of Harrisburg. The bridge stretches 3,820 feet across the Susquehanna River and is the longest stone arch bridge in the world. The bridge is listed on the National Register of Historic Places, has been declared a national historic civil engineering landmark, and is still in use today.

Rockville Bridge, Harrisburg, Pa.

The Rockville Bridge has 48 stone arches and was built by Drake and Stratton for the Pennsylvania Railroad as a connection of its railroad line from Philadelphia to Pittsburgh. This postcard is postmarked July 24, 1907.

CROSSROADS OF COMMERCE

The first bridge at Rockville was a one-track wooden bridge built in 1849. The second bridge at this location was a two-track iron bridge built in 1877. This third bridge is a four-track stone arch bridge built in 1902.

The First Train Crossing Rockville Bridge, longest stone bridge in the World Harrisburg, Pa.

This is a rare photograph of the first train to cross the new stone arch Rockville Bridge on Easter Sunday morning in 1902. Note the attention the event drew with sightseers on the bridge.

Two

Uncovered Wooden Bridges

View, Spangsville, Pa.

This is a simple footbridge near Spangsville in the Oley Valley part of Berks County. Several of this type of bridge were constructed by local farmers to get to their fields that were separated by creeks and streams. This type of bridge is considered a stringer bridge and does not have a truss for additional support. Because of the lack of a truss, the bridge is starting to sag.

The stringer bridge on the left is over a canal lock of the Lehigh Canal, and the stringer bridge on the right is over a feeder stream. The scene is between Bethlehem and Allentown in Lehigh County. The lockkeeper's house can be seen to the left of the canal lock.

Before wooden covered bridges were built, wooden bridges were uncovered. The problem with uncovered wooden bridges was that their trusses were exposed to the weather and their life expectancy was only about 10 to 12 years. The bridge on this postcard is a simple king post truss bridge that was located over the Wyomissing Creek near Reading. *Wyomissing* is an old Native American word meaning "place of long fish."

Bridge at East Titusville, Pa.

The wooden open bridge in this photograph was at East Titusville in southeastern Crawford County. Note the daring young man standing on the railing without holding on. Bridges such as this were common and were built by the railroad to avoid railroad crossings. These bridges usually had steep wooden approaches and tall wooden piers, and the wood was covered with a type of creosote that protected the wood from the elements. This postcard is postmarked July 7, 1909.

This short wooden open-span bridge was located in Hickory in northern Washington County. The bridge was constructed using a king post truss, which is considered to be the most elementary truss system in wooden bridge building. It is said that the triangle is the strongest geometric shape. A king post truss is made of a triangle on either side of a center post. This bridge was not covered, however, and the exposed wood was prone to develop wood rot. Note that the diagonal beam on the right is developing a split in the wood, the diagonal beam on the left is starting to deteriorate at its base, and the bridge is starting to sag. Even though the bridge is roofless, there is a height restriction on the bridge due to a cross supporting beam.

This is an open-deck wooden bridge over the Schuylkill Canal above Hamburg. Notice the canal lock gates just under the bridge. It was at this point that the canal towpath changed from one side of the canal to the other. The mules pulling the barges used the bridge to cross over the canal.

L. B. HERR PRINT   THE BRIDGES AT PEQUEA, PA.

The bridge on the right is the Samuel Harnish Sawmill Bridge, built about 1904 near Pequea in southern Lancaster County. Two covered bridges previously located at this spot were destroyed by floodwaters in 1902 and 1904, so it was decided to put up an uncovered bridge and expect that it would be washed out again. This bridge stood until 1913 when it was replaced with an iron bridge. The bridge on the left is a stone arch railroad bridge.

Temporary Bridge over Schuylkill River, Mont Clare, Pa., and P. & R. Station, Phoenixville, Pa.

This is a photograph of a temporary bridge over the Schuylkill River between Mont Clare in Montgomery County and Phoenixville in Chester County. The temporary bridge was put up after a covered bridge was destroyed by fire in 1915 (the one pier of the covered bridge can be seen on the right). Photographs of temporary bridges are rather rare because the bridges were usually only in existence for a short period of time until a permanent bridge could be built, and they were not often photographed because they were simple in design.

This is a boxed pony truss wooden bridge at Powell in south-central Bradford County. If a wooden bridge itself was not covered, quite often the truss would be covered or enclosed to protect it from the elements and prolong the life of the bridge.

Three

COVERED
WOODEN BRIDGES

The Carmen covered bridge was built in the 1870s over the Conneaut Creek east of Springfield in Erie County. This multiple king post truss bridge was unpainted for most of the years of its existence. Note the advertisement for the Stines and Wingate Clothing Store, a clothing store that was well known for its $10 suits. The bridge was destroyed by fire on April 19, 1996. (Joseph Conwill.)

515 Covered Bridge over Conewango, Russell, Pa.

The Russell Bridge crossed the Conewango Creek in northeastern Warren County. The bridge was built during 1827 and 1828 and was removed in 1937. Note the fancy white fencing along the pedestrian walkway. Also take note of the advertisement and the kids at the entrance of the bridge.

This photograph was taken from the opposite end of the Russell Bridge in the mid–1930s and gives a different impression of the bridge. The bridge seems to have been neglected and seems to be in need of paint. Note the sign on the wooden post stating, "This bridge unsafe cross at your own risk."

The Emlenton covered bridge was built over the Allegheny River at Emlenton in Venango County in 1856. The cost of construction of the bridge was $16,000. Note the hardware store with the white-stepped false front just to the right of the bridge in this 1872 photograph. The bridge was destroyed by a flood in 1883. The town was named after Hannah Emlen, wife of town's founder Joseph M. Fox.

This covered bridge was sometimes referred to as the "Black Bridge" because of the dark color of the bridge siding. The bridge was located at the Carnegie Steel Mill and Furnaces at New Castle. This Lawrence County bridge was built in 1851 and was removed in 1913.

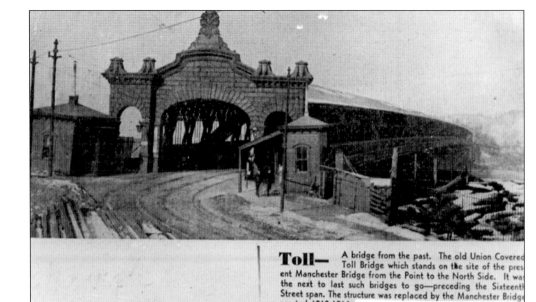

Toll— A bridge from the past. The old Union Covered Toll Bridge which stands on the site of the present Manchester Bridge from the Point to the North Side. It was the next to last such bridges to go—preceding the Sixteenth Street span. The structure was replaced by the Manchester Bridge erected 1912-1914.

The 1875 Union covered bridge over the Allegheny River in Pittsburgh served both trolley and roadway traffic. The portals were made of hand-carved wooden blocks that were supposed to resemble a fake stone facing. There was also an old tollbooth at the entrance to the bridge. This Howe truss covered bridge was removed in 1907.

The Brownsville covered bridge was built between Fayette and Washington Counties on the National Road in 1833. Before the covered bridge was built, there was a ferry crossing the Monongahela River at this point. It was a three-lane bridge, with two lanes for traffic and one lane for pedestrians, and was removed in 1922. The town of Brownsville got its name from a local landowner by the name of Thomas Brown.

Old River Bridge, Saltsburg, Pa.

The Saltsburg covered bridge crossed the Kiskiminetas River between Indiana and Westmoreland Counties at Saltsburg. Absalom Woodward built this two-span, double-barrel bridge in 1842 for a cost of $10,000. Note the many posters on the portal of the bridge. Covered bridges often served as early billboards for local events.

Burning of Covered Bridge 1922
Saltsburg, Pa.

On June 8, 1922, the Saltsburg covered bridge was destroyed by fire. Note the Burr arches and the charred wood on this view looking downstream. The Indiana County community of Saltsburg was named for its early salt industry.

Bridge at New Alexandria, Pa.

The New Alexandria covered bridge was built in 1832 over the Loyalhanna Creek in Westmoreland County, 30 miles east of Pittsburgh. The covered bridge was part of the old William Penn Highway (Route 22) that ran from Pittsburgh to New York City and, in parts, paralleled the Pennsylvania Railroad. This photograph was taken on March 21, 1912, during a significant rise in the level of the creek. Quite a few of the town's brave men walked onto the bridge to observe the high water. The covered bridge was replaced in 1921.

Old Wooden Bridge across Clarion River, near Clarion, Pa.

A good example of the Burr arch truss can be found in this postcard of a covered bridge over the Clarion River near Clarion. The Burr truss included an arch combined with a series of uprights and diagonals connecting the upper and lower chords. The land in this area was originally inhabited by the Allegwi Indian tribe, who were supposed to be people of gigantic stature.

"THE OLD COVERED BRIDGE" (ONLY ONE IN CLEARFIELD COUNTY) CURWENSVILLE, PA.

This could fall into the category of either a bridge postcard or a cow postcard. The covered bridge in this photograph was built in 1834 in the town of Curwensville in Clearfield County. Curwensville was named after John Curwen, a large landholder in the area. Clearfield County got its name from large local clearings in the middle of dense forests in this part of the state. The bridge stood until 1951. The cow did not last nearly as long, especially standing that close to the railroad tracks.

INTERIOR OF COVERED BRIDGE OVER JUNIATA RIVER. BUILT 1818. LINCOLN HIGHWAY. JUNIATA CROSSINGS.

This two-span covered bridge was in southern Pennsylvania one mile west of Breezewood in Bedford County and was originally built as a two-lane bridge. In the early 1900s, one span of the bridge was washed out during a flood. When the replacement span was built, it only had one lane. The other span remained a two-lane span. When traveling over the bridge from the single-lane part of the bridge to the double-lane part of the bridge one was confronted with rather dangerous center wooden beams separating the two lanes.

In another view of the Lincoln Highway (Route 30) bridge one mile west of Breezewood, a car can be seen coming out of the bridge. This Juniata River crossing was built in 1818 and was destroyed by a flood in 1936. Next to the bridge is the Stone Lodge, built around 1812, where such famous people as Abraham Lincoln, P. T. Barnum, and Zachary Taylor slept. The name Bedford County comes from Fort Bedford, which was a nearby fort built for the French and Indian War.

This two-lane Tioga County covered bridge was built in 1832 near the town of Tioga. There is an iron bridge over a railroad that can be seen by looking through the covered bridge. It was not unusual for railroad tracks to be laid along the banks of streams. This Burr truss covered bridge was removed in 1931. The postcard is postmarked March 3, 1914.

River Bridge, Looking South, Thompsontown, Pa.

The Thompsontown covered bridge crossed the Juniata River near Thompsontown in eastern Juniata County. The bridge was built during 1857 and 1858 and consisted of a four-span covered bridge and a one-span open approach bridge. Even though the bridge seems to have sufficient height in the photograph, a flood destroyed the bridge in 1936. Thompsontown was named after William Thompson, who settled and laid out the town that was once part of Mifflin County. On March 2, 1831, Juniata County was created from part of Mifflin County.

The Port Royal covered bridge was built in 1892 over the Tuscarora Creek near Port Royal in Juniata County. The bridge stood until three of its four spans were washed out by a flood on St. Patrick's Day in 1936. Port Royal was once known as Perrysville, named after Commodore Oliver Hazard Perry. The town was later named Port Royal to match the name of the local post office.

Old Covered Bridge, Watrous, Pa.

This one-span covered bridge was located in the town of Watrous in Tioga County. The Burr truss bridge was built in 1854 and crossed Pine Creek. Note the oil derricks in the background. The bridge was removed in 1936. Tioga County got its name from a tribe of Seneca Indians by the same name who once lived in this area.

Bridge and Mill, Bridge over 100 years old, Middleburg, Pa.

On Sunday mornings after church or on Sunday afternoons, bridges were often gathering places for kids. Notice the row of kids sitting on the abutment to the bridge. Quite often bridges were built near mills to allow people to get to and from the mills. People came to mills not only to buy and sell goods but also to catch up on news. Mills were the early gathering places to go where one could find a newspaper and exchange gossip. This is the Franklin Roller Mill and bridge near Middleburg in Snyder County.

This is the remains of a covered bridge at Mifflintown in Juniata County after a flood in June 1889 destroyed the bridge. This flood was caused by the same storm that caused the Johnstown Flood and dumped 6 to 10 inches of rain in 24 hours over Pennsylvania. The building in the middle of the photograph is the covered bridge tollhouse. Since the bridge was a toll bridge, the tollgates are still seen attached to the portal of the bridge.

The Sereno covered bridge was built over Little Fishing Creek between Pine and Greenwood Townships in Columbia County. A window was cut in the side of the bridge for visibility of oncoming traffic.

The Newburg covered bridge was built in 1834 over the Conodoguinet Creek in Cumberland County. This 100-foot-long Burr arch truss bridge was replaced about 1933. *Conodoguinet* is a Native American word meaning "a long way with many bends."

Quigley's Twin Bridges were located near Newburg in Cumberland County. Both bridges were built in 1824 and were Burr truss bridges. One bridge was across the Conodoguinet Creek and the other bridge was across a millrace. Note the stepped portal common to Cumberland County covered bridges. Also note the forest of telephone poles between the bridges. Both bridges were removed in 1947.

Watt's Bridge was built in 1890 over the Conodoguinet Creek in Cumberland County. The two-span, 235-foot-long Burr arch truss bridge was destroyed by fire in 1970. Although the progression seems backward, an iron bridge existed at this location before the covered bridge was built. The covered bridge was built for half the price of the original iron bridge. (James P. Bissett.)

Orr's Bridge was built in 1855 by John Finley at a cost of $4,973. The two-span, 337-foot-long Burr truss bridge was located over the Conodoguinet Creek west of Camp Hill. This Cumberland County bridge was replaced in 1957. The bridge got its name from John Orr, who owned the land on one side of the creek.

Eyster's or Oyster's covered bridge was located over the Conodoguinet Creek in East Pennsboro Township in Cumberland County. The three-span, 408-foot-long Burr truss bridge was built in 1881 and was destroyed by fire in 1958. The bridge was named for a nearby mill. (Vera H. Wagner.)

This is the Alexander covered bridge over the Conodoguinet Creek near Carlisle in Cumberland County. The first covered bridge at this location was built in 1834 by Samuel Alexander for $1,300. The two-span covered bridge shown was the second covered bridge at this location and was built in 1878. One span of the 1878 covered bridge burned on August 26, 1952, while the other span was washed away one month later. (D. W. Thompson.)

The Engleside covered bridge crossed the Conestoga Creek northeast of New Danville in southern Lancaster County. The bridge was built in 1824 and was named after the nearby Engleside Mill. This was a 317-foot-long, two-span Burr truss bridge that was replaced in 1901. (James P. Papez.)

LITTLE CHICKIES CREEK, MT. JOY, PA.

This covered bridge was located over Little Chickies Creek near Mount Joy in Lancaster County. The postcard itself is more interesting than the actual photograph. This is an early-1900s postcard where the back of the postcard was not divided and the message had to be written on the front of the card. Messages had to be short.

This is a photograph taken from Indian Hill in southern Lancaster County and shows the beautiful countryside in that area of Pennsylvania. Lancaster County was formed from part of Chester County on May 10, 1729. The bridge in the middle of the photograph is the Old Factory Bridge over the Conestoga Creek.

Old Factory Bridge, Williamson Park, Lancaster, Pa.

The Old Factory Bridge took its name from a nearby factory that had been at various times a silk mill, a match factory, a fulling mill, a woolen mill, and a cork factory. The two-span covered bridge was built in 1853 by Elias McMellen and was removed in 1948. The first inhabitants of this area were a peaceful tribe of Native Americans known as the Susquehannocks, whose name meant "people of the muddy river."

Covered Bridge near Connellsville, Pa.

The Pine Grove Forge covered bridge is located over the Octoraro Creek between Lancaster and Chester Counties. The two–span, 199–foot–long Burr arch truss bridge was built in 1884 at a cost of $4,295. The bridge was named for a nearby forge and is still in use. The postcard was mislabeled "near Connellsville."

This was the Stoneroad covered bridge and mill near the western end of the city of Lancaster. The multi–king post truss bridge was built in 1868 and was destroyed by the flood of 1972. While some bridges were located near a mill, this bridge was all but against the mill.

This postcard shows a perfect reflection of a covered bridge over Muncy Creek in Muncy in Lycoming County. If the postcard is rotated 180 degrees, the image of the bridge is just as clear. *Lycoming* is a Delaware Indian word meaning "sandy or gravelly creek."

This 1855 covered bridge was built over the Wyalusing Creek at Camptown in Bradford County. While most bridges had a level roofline, this bridge had a very unusual rise in its roofline. This 1915 photograph shows the bridge was washed out by a flood and came to rest on dry land.

COVERED BRIDGE, Bartonsville, Pa.

This covered bridge was located near Bartonsville in Monroe County. Note the old car going across the bridge, the unusual outcropping of the abutment wall, and the posters attached to the portal of the bridge. Also, on the other side of the bridge, part of a railroad crossing sign can be seen.

LEHIGHTON & WEISSPORT BRIDGE CROSSING THE LEHIGH RIVER, UNTIL 1890.

This was the Lehighton and Weissport covered bridge connecting the two towns over the Lehigh River. The two-span Carbon County Burr truss arch bridge was replaced with an iron bridge in 1890. Carbon County got its name from the large amounts of coal deposits found in this part of the state.

Old Ferry Landing, Bethlehem, Pa.

This covered bridge crossed the Lehigh River and connected Bethlehem and South Bethlehem. The docks in the foreground were originally used for the ferry that had connected Bethlehem and South Bethlehem before the bridge was built.

3759—Covered Bridge over Lehigh River, Bethlehem, Pa.

This is a postcard of the same bridge between Bethlehem and South Bethlehem, only from the opposite side of the river. The two-lane Burr truss bridge had two sidewalks and was built in 1841. Note the openness of the bridge, showing the truss work. The bridge was replaced in 1921.

This is an aerial view looking from South Bethlehem to Bethlehem. Not only does one see the covered bridge, but there is also a trolley bridge in the foreground. The building on the right is the Pacific Hotel.

The Pacific Hotel was located in South Bethlehem. A trolley bridge is on the left of the hotel, the Bethlehem–South Bethlehem covered bridge is on the right of the hotel, and railroad tracks are in front of the hotel. No quiet night's sleep here.

View along the Lehigh showing old wooden Bridge.
Easton, Pa.

This covered bridge connected Easton and Glendon in Northampton County. The three-span covered bridge was built in 1831 over the Lehigh River. Notice the lack of siding on this bridge. The photograph might have been taken when the bridge was being repaired or replaced. The town of Glendon grew up around and was named after the Glendon Iron Works.

NO. 1.   SHIMERSVILLE, PA.

The two-span Shimersville covered bridge was built over the Saucon Creek in Northampton County. Note the two-span iron trolley bridge located right next to the covered bridge. The covered bridge was removed in 1897.

46

The Birdsboro covered bridge was built during 1844 and 1845 over the Schuylkill River several miles south of Reading in Berks County. Note the telephone poles on the roof of the bridge and the advertisements on the portal of the bridge. The covered bridge was purposefully destroyed by fire in 1926.

Stoudt's Ferry Bridge was built by the Schuylkill Navigation Company for the purpose of carrying its mules over the Schuylkill River. It was here that the canal towpath crossed over the river. There were cloverleafs at each end of the bridge for the mule paths. This was one of the first uses of a traffic cloverleaf employed in the state of Pennsylvania. The bridge was also a toll bridge for local vehicular traffic. The tollhouse can be seen to the left of the bridge on the hillside.

Stoudt's Ferry Bridge was built six and a half miles north of Reading and was the longest single-span covered bridge built in Berks County with a span of 240 feet measured portal to portal. The bridge was built between 1856 and 1857. Notice the orchard in the background.

Stoudt Ferry Bridge across the Schuylkill River, Snyder Fry and Rick Orchards

Stoudt's Ferry Bridge had three lanes—two outer lanes that were mule paths for the Schuylkill Canal and a middle lane that was used for regular traffic. In this photograph, taken in the 1940s, only tar paper covered the roof. Over time the tar paper became loose and the bridge became exposed to rain and snow. Eventually the wood rotted and the bridge collapsed in 1948.

Bridge Crossing Maiden Creek at Berkley,   Reading, Pa.

This was Schlegel's Bridge located over the Maiden Creek at Berkley between Reading and Leesport in Berks County. The bridge was built in 1869 and was in existence until 1922. This roadway is now a four-lane divided highway.

Bridge at Berkley above Reading, Pa.

This is a German hand-painted and enhanced version of Schlegel's Bridge. Notice that women were added to the approach to the bridge and that the bridge beams, the arches, and the siding were accented so that they would stand out. During the early 1900s, a postcard company in Germany employed women to hand paint American postcards. The German versions of the postcards usually had more detail and had more color than the original American versions.

49

Leize's Bridge was built in 1833, four miles north of Reading. The two-span, 336-foot-long Burr truss bridge crossed the Schuylkill River. Old records state that in 1862 on a snowy winter day, Charles Karins was paid $1 for putting snow on the bridge for the passage of sleighs.

In its early years, Leize's Bridge was a toll bridge that charged 1¢ for foot passengers, 5¢ for a horse and truck, and 10¢ for a horse and carriage. On June 18, 1952, the bridge was destroyed by fire under suspicious circumstances.

13. Old State Bridge—Stateville Hotel, Bernville & Reading Stage Route

This is the only known photograph of the Blue Marsh covered bridge. The bridge was built in 1846 over the Tulpehocken Creek in the village of Blue Marsh just north of Reading. The word *Tulpehocken* comes from the Native American word *Tulpewihaki*, meaning "land of the turtles." The bridge had the nickname of "Old State Bridge" because the general area around the bridge was sometimes referred to as Stateville. The bridge was replaced by an iron one in 1909.

The Covered Bridge Across The Manatawny. In the Oley Valley in Beautiful Berks, near Earlville, Berks County, Pennsylvania.

The Earlville covered bridge was originally built in 1852 as an uncovered bridge because of a shortage of lumber. It was not until four years later that the sides were raised and a roof was put on the bridge. The line running the length of the bridge about halfway up the side shows where the upper addition was made to the bridge.

The Earlville covered bridge crossed the Manatawny Creek at Earlville near the village of Yellow House. The local Native Americans of the area called the stream Menhaltanik, meaning "where we drank liquor." Many happy evenings must have been spent by the Native Americans on the banks of this creek.

The Earlville Bridge Crossing the Manatawny in Beautiful Berks. Named By The Indians "Menhaltanink." Near Earlville, Berks County, Pennsylvania.

In all color postcards of this covered bridge, the bridge appears faded or discolored. It was not until old courthouse records were found that it was revealed that the bridge was actually painted pale yellow. The hotel and several houses in Yellow House were also painted pale yellow. This was presumably to promote the village of Yellow House.

No. 3 Covered Bridge, Schwenksville, Pa.

This is an early postcard of a two-span covered bridge near Schwenksville in Montgomery County. The large old tree in the foreground probably gets more attention than the bridge. Note the large amount of the tree's root system that is exposed.

This is a photograph of a covered bridge at Zieglersville in Montgomery County. The postcard is a very early postcard from the 1901 to 1907 undivided-back era of postcards. Since the back was not divided, messages were not allowed to be written on the back. All messages had to be written on the front of the card. In this case, notice how every available space on the card was used to write the message.

Covered Bridge over the Perkiomen Creek, Oaks, Pa.

The 218-foot-long Oaks covered bridge was built in 1833 over the Perkiomen Creek at Oaks in Montgomery County. The Schuylkill Canal had canal locks at Oaks. The village of Oaks is named after Thomas Oakes, the designer of the Schuylkill Canal.

Iron Bridge over Perkiomen Creek, Oaks, Pa.

In this early-1920s photograph of the Oaks covered bridge, a car is seen coming out of the covered bridge that crossed the Perkiomen Creek and approaching an iron bridge that was across railroad tracks. The word *Perkiomen* comes from the Native American word *Pakihmomink*, meaning "place of cranberries." The covered bridge was removed in 1931.

ONLY COVERED BRIDGE IN MONTGOMERY COUNTY. PA.

Montgomery County once had over 30 covered bridges. This was Knight's Road covered bridge, the last remaining covered bridge in Montgomery County until it was removed in 1956. This Town truss bridge crossed the Perkiomen Creek near Markley's Mill. This postcard was postmarked September 3, 1948, and was mailed from Sumneytown to Philadelphia.

This is the Delphi Bridge built by the Reading Railroad east of Zieglersville in Montgomery County. Wooden roofed railroad bridges were rather rare in this area because the roofs often caught on fire from the embers of the steam trains. Most of these bridges ended up having tall sides and open roofs after fire burned off the original roofs. This covered bridge was replaced in 1910.

The Parkerford three-span Town truss covered bridge was over the Schuylkill River between Linfield in Montgomery County and Parkerford in Chester County. Parkerford was a small town that derived its name from a ford that was in the river at this location prior to the covered bridge being built in 1849.

The tollhouse (above right) for the 375-foot-long Parkerford covered bridge was on the Linfield side of the Schuylkill River. The bridge was freed from charging tolls in 1891, and the bridge was removed in 1932. *Schuylkill* is a Dutch word meaning "hidden stream."

Bridge over the Schuylkill River at Norristown, Pa.

The Dekalb Street covered bridge crossed the Schuylkill River at Norristown. The bridge was built in 1829 by Lawrence Corson. The bridge had three lanes—two outside lanes for vehicular traffic and one center lane for pedestrians. The bridge was replaced in 1924.

Jefferi's Ford, route of British Army Battle of Brandywine, Sept. 11, 1777

The Jefferi's Ford covered bridge was another bridge named for a former ford. Joseph Elliott built this bridge in 1833 at a cost of $2,789. This was the route of the British army during the Battle of Brandywine in 1777, 56 years before the bridge was built. The bridge was demolished in 1934.

The advertisement "Smith's Red Cross Balsam, for Coughs, Colds, and Sore Throat, 25¢, Parkesburg, Chester Co, Pa" was written directly on a photograph. The photograph was then made into a postcard. To some, this was a good way of advertising, while to others who wanted to enjoy the photograph, it was distracting. Parkesburg is in western Chester County.

Sugars Bridge, on the Brandywine, near West Chester, Pa.

Sugar's Bridge was located over the East Branch of the Brandywine Creek east of West Chester. The bridge took its name from Sugar's Ford, which was the only way to cross the creek in this area before the covered bridge was built. The ford got its name from William Sugar, a local farmer who owned the land on one side of the creek. The bridge was replaced in 1929.

The Knox covered bridge is located over Valley Creek in Valley Forge National Park. Robert Russell built the covered bridge in 1865 at a cost of $1,170. Some say the name of the bridge comes from Philander C. Knox, a senator from Pennsylvania who owned 256 acres of land near the covered bridge. The bridge is painted white, has a side opening running the entire length of the bridge, and is still in use.

Shaw's Bridge was built in 1862 over the East Branch of the Brandywine Creek in Chester County. Nathan Y. Jester built the bridge at a cost of $2,130. The bridge was named after Francis and William Shaw, who owned the land on the western side of the creek. Prior to the bridge being built, there was a ford at this location called Buffington's Ford, named after William Buffington, who, at that time, owned land in the area. The bridge was burned down by vandals in 1953.

Neely's Bridge was located near Bowman's Hill near New Hope in Bucks County. This Town truss bridge was named after Neely's Grist Mill, which was located nearby. The bridge crossed Pidcock Creek, a creek that was named after John Pidcock, who was the first settler at the mouth of the creek. The bridge was removed in 1935.

Seeds Bridge was built in 1834 by Wilson Buffington over the West Branch of the Brandywine Creek in Chester County. George and Emmor Seeds, who were local farmers, lead the petition to have a bridge built at this site and the bridge took their name. The three-span, 270-foot-long Burr truss bridge was replaced in 1932.

Beatty's Hollow covered bridge was located over Crum Creek near Media in Delaware County. The rustic setting and leaves on the ground gave charm to this Burr truss covered bridge postcard. This bridge was one of 10 covered bridges over Crum Creek in Delaware County. Delaware County was created in 1789 from part of Chester County and is named for the Delaware River.

The Leiper Quarry covered bridge was originally a two-lane bridge. The left half of the bridge carried vehicular traffic while the right half of the bridge carried tracks for the Leiper Railway. The Leiper Railway was used to carry stone from the Leiper Quarry over Crum Creek to a stone mill. The heavy loads carried by the trains started to make the railway side of the bridge sag. Eventually that half of the bridge was removed. This bridge was located near Swarthmore in Delaware County.

The Portland-Columbia Bridge crossed the Delaware River between Portland, Pennsylvania, and Columbia, New Jersey. The four-span Burr arch truss bridge had a length of 775 feet.

The Portland-Columbia Bridge was built in 1869 by Charles Kellogg at a cost of $46,600. In this view from the Pennsylvania side of the Delaware River, the former tollhouse can be seen against the bridge on the left side of the entrance. For many years, a purple martin house on a long pole gave a uniqueness to the bridge that can be seen in this photograph on the right side of the entrance to the bridge.

Entrance, Covered Bridge, Columbia, N. J.

This is the view of the Portland–Columbia Bridge from the New Jersey side of the Delaware River. The bridge was destroyed by a flood in 1955.

"Old Toll Bridge" Portland, Pa.

Advertisements were sometimes painted on the sides of a bridge to promote various products. On the Portland-Columbia Bridge is the advertisement "Sozodont for the Teeth and Breath." Sozodont was a powder dentifrice whose slogan was "Good for bad teeth, not bad for good teeth." During another period of time, the bridge had a "Coca Cola, sold everywhere, 5¢" advertisement painted on its side.

**Covered Bridge across the Delaware River, Frenchtown, NJ — Uhlerstown, PA
Washed out during Flood of October 10, 1903**

The Alexandria covered bridge crossed the Delaware River between Uhlerstown, Pennsylvania, and Frenchtown, New Jersey. The six-span, 962-foot-long bridge was built in 1844 for a cost of $20,000. This photograph shows the bridge after it was destroyed by a flood on October 10, 1903. (Washington Crossing Card Collectors Club.)

The West Branch of the Susquehanna River and the North Branch of the Susquehanna River come together in the town of Northumberland. In this postcard, in the foreground is a covered vehicular bridge over the West Branch of the Susquehanna River. In the background are two bridges over the North Branch of the Susquehanna River. The lower bridge was a railroad bridge while the upper bridge was a vehicular bridge.

Old Covered Bridge, Built 1841, Athens, Pa.

This three-span covered bridge was built in 1841 over the North Branch of the Susquehanna River in Athens in Bradford County. Athens is about two miles south of the New York border. On early maps from the 1600s, Susquehanna was originally spelled "Sasquesahanough."

Old Coverd Bridge, East Entrance, Athens, Pa.

The approaches to the Athens covered bridge, although fairly wide, were quite steep. This photograph is also a reminder that the roads back in the early 1900s were dirt roads.

65

The Towanda covered bridge crossed the North Branch of the Susquehanna River in the town of Towanda in Bradford County. Towanda is about 15 miles south of Athens. This Burr arch truss covered bridge was built in 1832 by John Bottom. One span of the bridge was destroyed by fire twice in its lifetime and rebuilt. This postcard is postmarked September 23, 1907.

The Towanda covered bridge was sometimes referred to as the "Old Wagon Bridge" to differentiate the bridge from a nearby railroad bridge. This bridge was for vehicular traffic, such as wagons, and was not used for railroad traffic. Notice the tollhouse at the entrance to the bridge. The bridge was removed in 1914.

A covered bridge was built in 1829 over the North Branch of the Susquehanna River between Danville in Montour County and Riverside in Northumberland County. The bridge had seven spans and was 1,350 feet long. This photograph shows the bridge being destroyed by an ice jam on March 9, 1904.

This was the 1836 Berwick-Nescopeck covered bridge over the North Branch of the Susquehanna River between Berwick in Columbia County and Nescopeck in Luzerne County. This was the second covered bridge at this location, replacing Theodore Burr's earlier 1813–1814 covered bridge that was washed out during a flood in 1835. In the early years, tolls were charged to cross the bridge. Schoolchildren going to and from school and also funeral attendees were exempt from paying tolls to cross the bridge.

OLD AND NEW BERWICK-NESCOPECK BRIDGES, PA. 768

Published by Sterling Store

This postcard shows both Berwick-Nescopeck bridges, the earlier 1836 covered bridge and the 1905 iron replacement bridge. Both bridges were comprised of six spans. The postcard is postmarked December 13, 1907, and the message on the back of the postcard reads, "This is the next bridge above the damaged Mifflinville bridge which was similar in type. One span of iron bridge and one span of false bridge went down at Mifflinville. The river rose all together about 12 feet since the rain. Water is now falling. No bodies can be taken out until low water. Great shock to community. However only three were from this vicinity. None of my members."

Covered Bridge, Over Susquehanna River, Lock Haven, Pa.

In 1852, the Lock Haven covered bridge was built over the West Branch of the Susquehanna River in the town of Lock Haven. Lock Haven got its name because the Pennsylvania Canal constructed a canal lock at this location and from the river's safe haven at this location.

ONE OF THE OLDEST BRIDGES IN THE STATE, CROSSING SUSQUEHANNA RIVER, LOCK HAVEN, PA.

The Lock Haven covered bridge had four spans and a length of 840 feet. The Burr truss arch bridge also had a separate sidewalk for pedestrians. In the earlier years, the sidewalk was used by canal mules to cross the river at this point. This Clinton County crossing caught on fire and burned in 1919.

The Lewisburg covered bridge was built over the West Branch of the Susquehanna River between Union and Northumberland Counties. The eight-span bridge was built in 1868 at a cost of $140,000 and was shared by the Spruce Creek and Center Railroad, a trolley line, and wagon and pedestrian traffic.

Old Covered Bridge at Lewisburg, Pa.

The Lewisburg covered bridge later became part of the Pennsylvania Railroad but was still shared by both the Pennsylvania Railroad and vehicular traffic. In 1902, the bridge was declared unsafe, and in 1910, the bridge was demolished after two newer bridges were built—one for the railroad and one for vehicular traffic.

This was Clarks Ferry covered bridge over the Susquehanna River north of Harrisburg connecting Dauphin and Perry Counties. The photograph shows the north, or upper, side of the bridge looking west. The original covered bridge was built in 1829 as a Town truss bridge. In 1836, it was rebuilt as a Burr truss bridge, and in the early years, it was a toll bridge. (Vera H. Wagner.)

The 1829 Clarks Ferry covered bridge replaced a ferry crossing at the site that was in operation since the 1760s. The ferry was put back into temporary service when the bridge was washed out in a flood. The bridge had two roadway lanes and an outside towpath. The photograph was taken looking east from the upstream side. The covered bridge was removed in 1925 and replaced with a reinforced concrete bridge.

The Camelback Bridge was built by Theodore Burr between 1812 and 1817 over the Susquehanna River at Harrisburg. The bridge had two traffic lanes and two walkways. (Theodore Burr Covered Bridge Society of Pennsylvania.)

The Camelback Bridge was actually two separate bridges that set down on an island in the middle of the Susquehanna River. The eastern span was removed in 1902, and the western span, shown above, was removed in 1903. The bridge got its name from the unusual humplike shape of the western span.

No. 16—The First Bridge. Columbia. Pa. Destroyed by Ice. 1832   RICHARDS & ECKMAN

This postcard is a drawing of the first Columbia-Wrightsville covered bridge. The bridge was built during 1813 and 1814 by Jonathan Wolcott at a cost of $231,771. With 28 spans and a length of 5,678 feet, the bridge was the longest covered bridge ever built. The bridge was destroyed by an ice jam in the river on February 5, 1832.

RICHARDS & ECKMAN, PUBLISHERS

No 10—Columbia. Pa.. Bridge. burned down during Civil War. June 30. 1863

The second Columbia-Wrightsville covered bridge was completed in 1834. During the Civil War, Union troops tried to blow up one of the spans with dynamite to prevent the Confederate army from advancing. However, the dynamite was not strong enough, so fire was set to one of the spans. The fire spread quickly, and the entire bridge was destroyed on June 30, 1863. The bridge was the only way over the river for 25 miles to the north or south of Wrightsville.

Columbia Bridge, destroyed by Cyclone, Columbia, Pa.

The Pennsylvania Railroad bought the rights to construct the third Columbia-Wrightsville covered bridge. Construction was started in 1868, and the bridge was opened in 1870. The bridge used the same piers as the previous bridge, and the railroad shared the bridge with roadway traffic. This photograph was taken from the Wrightsville side of the river looking toward Columbia.

No. 5.—Columbia, Pa., Bridge destroyed by cyclone.

The remains of the third Columbia-Wrightsville covered bridge over the Susquehanna River in central Pennsylvania can be seen here. This third bridge was still the longest covered bridge in the world with a length of 5,390 feet. It was destroyed by a windstorm in 1896.

Four

SUSPENSION BRIDGES

Pittsburgh was sometimes referred to as the "City of Bridges." This postcard shows five of the major bridges in downtown Pittsburgh. The bridge at the top on the left is the Point Bridge (once a suspension bridge) over the Monongahela River. The bridge at the top on the right is the Manchester Bridge (once a covered bridge). And the three bridges on the right starting from the top are the Sixth Street Bridge, the Seventh Street Bridge, and the Ninth Street Bridge. These three bridges, known as the Three Sisters, were built between 1925 and 1928 over the Allegheny River and are still in operation.

This 1911 photograph shows an old swinging suspension footbridge near Galeton. Galeton is in Pennsylvania's northern Potter County. As shown in the photograph, kids have always been attracted to swinging bridges. This postcard is postmarked August 9, 1911.

The Cable "Swinging Bridge"
Crossing over the Youghigeny River
Near Perryopolis, Pa.

This swinging footbridge crossed the Youghiogheny River near Perryopolis in northern Fayette County. While large highway suspension bridges leading into large cities were impressive, they were not as exciting to cross as were long swinging foot suspension bridges such as this one.

Upper Suspension Bridge and Lehigh River, Easton, Pa.

This was the Upper Suspension Bridge over the Lehigh River at Easton in Northampton County. The three-span bridge connected Dock Street to Glendon Street and was removed in 1955. The bridge is believed to have been one of the largest foot suspension bridges to have existed in Pennsylvania.

2759—Point Bridge and Coal Boats, Pittsburg, Pa.

Souvenir Post Card Co., New York and Berlin.

One of Pennsylvania's most famous suspension bridges was the Point Suspension Bridge built in 1877 over the Monongahela River at the Point in Pittsburgh. The bridge was built by the American Bridge Company for about $525,000. Note the coal barges filled with coal and the three steamboats on the river.

Point Suspension Bridge, Pittsburg. Pa.

This postcard from 1906 gives a closer view of the Point Suspension Bridge. It was 1,245 feet in length and had towers that were 180 feet high measured from the low water mark. The bridge was closed in 1924 and replaced in 1927.

Where the Allegheny and Monongahela Rivers join to form the Ohio.

The bridge in the foreground is the Point Suspension Bridge over the Monongahela River, while the wooden covered bridge in the background is the Union covered bridge over the Allegheny River. This scene is at the Point in Pittsburgh, where the Allegheny River and the Monongahela River come together to form the Ohio River.

This linen-era postcard shows the 1925–1926 Sixth Street Bridge over the Allegheny River in Pittsburgh. It is an unusual self-anchored suspension bridge with steel eyebar chain cables and a steel plate girder deck. This is the first suspension bridge in the United States that did not have heavy anchorages to hold the cable ends into the earth. Instead, the towers hold the ends apart. The length of the main span of the bridge is 442 feet. The bridge won the annual award by the American Institute of Steel Construction for the "most beautiful Steel Bridge of 1928."

The Monaca–Rochester suspension bridge was built in 1896 over the Ohio River between Rochester and Monaca near the mouth of the Beaver River in Butler County. The suspension bridge was in existence until 1930. Note the high elevated iron approaches to the suspension bridge.

This 1871 Warren County suspension bridge was on Hickory Street in Warren. The bridge was built by George W. Fischer of Elmira, New York, at a cost of almost $45,000. Prior to this suspension bridge, there was a wooden covered toll bridge at this location. This postcard is postmarked June 5, 1908.

The anchors to the suspension bridge in Warren were attached below these stone walls just beyond the entrance to the bridge. Usually anchors were sunk to a gravel bed below low water level. Bridge tolls were charged until 1895, and in 1918, the suspension bridge was replaced by a concrete arch bridge. Note the large towers pedestrians had to walk through to cross the bridge.

Robeling's Aqueduct between Lackawaxen, Pennsylvania, and Minisink Ford, New York, is the oldest existing wire suspension bridge in the United States. The 1847–1848 aqueduct was designed and built under the supervision of John A. Roebling, who is also known for building the Brooklyn Bridge. The 535-foot-long aqueduct carried the Delaware and Hudson Canal over the Delaware River. When the canal closed in 1898, the aqueduct was converted into a one-lane vehicular bridge. The aqueduct has been designated as a national historic landmark and also as a national civil engineering landmark.

In the beginning, this 1926 iron suspension bridge that connected Philadelphia with Camden, New Jersey, was simply referred to as the Delaware River Bridge. It was not until another iron suspension bridge, the Walt Whitman Bridge, was built in Philadelphia in 1956 that this bridge was renamed the Ben Franklin Bridge.

81

At the time of construction, the Ben Franklin Bridge was considered the world's largest suspension bridge with a total length of 1.81 miles and with towers reaching a height of 385 feet. There are six vehicular lanes, two high-speed track lanes, two trolley lanes, and two pedestrian lanes.

The Ben Franklin Bridge granite anchorages, to which the steel cables are attached, cover three-quarters of an acre. The two anchorages together required 216,000 tons of masonry. They are built 65 feet into the ground on the Philadelphia side and 105 feet into the ground on the New Jersey side. On the inside of the structure, the cables come down and splay apart into the actual anchorages. Both of these structures were originally designed to contain trolley stations, but that idea was not followed through with when the anchorages were finished.

Five

METAL BRIDGES

Shown in this photograph are the Hydetown Union Church and two typical iron bridges, one vehicular bridge and one trolley bridge at Hydetown in eastern Crawford County. Crawford County was named for William Crawford, who was an American soldier and land surveyor for George Washington. He fought in both the French and Indian War and the American Revolutionary War.

This postcard shows a car about to go over a metal arch truss bridge located on East Pine Street in Grove City in southeastern Mercer County. Note the glass light globes at the four corners of the bridge. Also note the fancy wrought iron fencing along the walkway.

This metal truss bridge at Clarion shows how early roadways sometimes followed the banks of a stream. This lead to sharp and sometimes hazardous 90-degree turns at the approaches to bridges. This was not a problem until cars were designed to go faster. Clarion County was formed in 1839 from the parent counties of Venango County and Armstrong County.

The Kinzua Viaduct was constructed in only 94 days. At the time of its construction in 1882, it was the highest railroad viaduct in the world at 302 feet. In 1975, the bridge was designated as a national civil engineering landmark. *Kinzua* is a Native American word meaning "waters of many and large fishes."

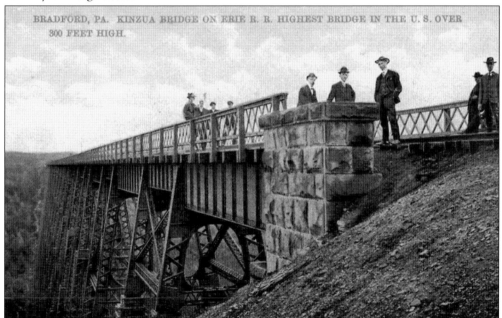

This is a closer look at the Kinzua Viaduct in McKean County. The iron bridge was rebuilt with steel in 1900 because of the increased weights of locomotives and their transportation loads. The 2,053-foot-long bridge was destroyed by a windstorm on July 21, 2003.

RAILROAD BRIDGE ACROSS TUNAUGWON RIVER, BRADFORD, PA.

This early railroad bridge was over the Tunungwant River, locally abbreviated and referred to as the "Tuna River," in the town of Bradford in northern McKean County. McKean County was formed in 1804 and named after Thomas McKean, who was the governor of Pennsylvania at that time. Even though trains make a lot of noise going over an iron bridge, the man sitting on the bank of this river does not seem to take notice of the train.

STATE STREET BRIDGE FROM SOUTH SIDE, OIL CITY, PA.

The three-span State Street Bridge crossed the Allegheny River in Oil City in central Venango County. In 1859 in Titusville in nearby Crawford County, Edwin Drake drilled Pennsylvania's first oil well. Soon oil drilling spread to Venango County, and, for many years, Oil City was known as the center of the petroleum industry. By the mid-1900s, Quaker State, Pennzoil, and Wolf's Head Oil Companies all had their headquarters located in Oil City.

The Lyndora trolley trestle bridge was located at Lyndora in central Butler County. In this photograph, the bridge appears to be brand-new because of the white appearance of the wooden decking and because of the proud conductor standing in front of the trolley and pointing to the bridge.

The East Mahoning Bridge was in Punxsutawney, a town located in Jefferson County northeast of Pittsburgh. The town is known for its yearly observance of Groundhog Day and is the home of Punxsutawney Phil. Note the trolley tracks passing over the bridge and through the town.

Beaver Falls had three metal bridges across the Beaver River connecting Beaver Falls to New Brighton. The bridge at the top of the photograph next to the falls is the Tenth Street vehicular bridge. The bridge in the center is a trolley bridge, and the one in the foreground is a Pennsylvania Railroad bridge.

R-1   P. & L. E. R. R. Bridge and Junction of Ohio and Beaver Rivers,

This impressive cantilever railroad bridge spanned the Ohio River in Beaver. The towns of Beaver and Rochester can be seen in the background. The bridge has the graceful shape of a suspension bridge while being built completely of metal. The bridge was built by A. R. Raymer for the Lake Erie Railroad in 1907. Note the steamboat making its way up the Ohio River.

The Kittanning Citizens Bridge was built over the Allegheny River in Kittanning in Armstrong County. This three-span vehicular bridge was built in either 1930 or 1932 depending on which marker is read. The bridge was filmed in a 2002 movie called *The Mothman Prophecies*. It shared the starring role along with Richard Gere.

The Panther Hollow Bridge crosses Panther Hollow Lake in Schenley Park in Pittsburgh. The bridge is a three-hinged deck arch bridge built in 1897 by Giuseppe Moretti. At the four corners of the bridge are bronze statues of mountain lions. The bridge took its name from the surrounding area that was known as a favorite living place of these animals.

The Smithfield Street Bridge was built by Gustav Lindenthal in 1883 over the Monongahela River in Pittsburgh using an unusual lenticular (lens-shaped) truss. The bridge is one of the oldest existing major steel truss bridges in the United States, is on the list of national historic civil engineering landmarks, and is still in use today. Note the steamboat sign on the roof of the building stating, "Excursion Season Now Open, $5.00 to Morgantown and return."

This is a view of the 1892 Sixth Street Bridge over the Allegheny River with the city of Pittsburgh in the background. This bridge replaced an 1857 suspension bridge built by John A. Roebling that was once described as "the most beautiful bridge in the world." A close inspection of the postcard shows trolleys, horse and wagons, and pedestrians using the bridge. This would place the time of the photograph in the early 1900s. The bridge was replaced in 1925 with a suspension bridge.

The Fort Pitt Bridge was constructed in Pittsburgh over the Monongahela River between 1956 and 1959. The bridge is considered a double-deck steel bowstring arch bridge and leads from the city to the Fort Pitt Tunnel. Fort Pitt was built in 1758 during the French and Indian War at what is now Pittsburgh.

During Pres. Thomas Jefferson's term in office, plans were made to build the National Road, the first federally funded highway. Between 1836 and 1839, the Dunlap Creek Bridge was built along the National Road in Brownsville in Washington County. The bridge is believed to be the first cast-iron bridge built in the United States and the oldest cast-iron bridge in the United States that is still in public use. The bridge has been designated as a national historic civil engineering landmark.

This postcard is postmarked August 5, 1910, and shows a metal bridge over the Youghiogheny River at Connellsville in northern Fayette County. The Youghiogheny River is a tributary of the Monongahela River. Located in a river valley southeast of here is Frank Lloyd Wright's Fallingwater.

This was the Big Rock Bridge in Franklin. On most bridges, vehicular traffic and trolley traffic shared the same roadway. In this unusual two-deck bridge, the lower level of the bridge was for vehicular traffic while the upper level of the bridge was for trolley traffic.

Trolley Bridge over the Juanita River, Tyrone, Pa.

The single-track Tyrone metal truss trolley bridge crossed the Juniata River in northern Blair County. A trolley can be seen approaching the bridge in the distance. One of the first settlements in the area now known as Blair County was a Delaware Indian village called Assunnepachla. *Juniata* is a Native American name meaning "people of the standing stone."

RED BRIDGE OVER P. R. R. YARDS. ALTOONA, PA.

The so-called Red Bridge was built by the Pennsylvania Railroad over its yards in Altoona. The railroad owned land in the Altoona area that covered 242 acres. During its peak in the mid-1920s, over 20,000 people were employed by the railroad in the Altoona area. Altoona's name comes from the Cherokee word *Allatoona*, which means "the high lands of great worth."

Here is an unusual pair of Baltimore (Pratt) truss railroad bridges near Hyndman in southwestern Bedford County. In 1877, when the Baltimore and Ohio Railroad came through what was then called Bridgeport, the town was renamed Hyndman in honor of the Baltimore and Ohio Connellsville Division railroad superintendent E. K. Hyndman.

This is a typical metal through truss bridge near Carlisle in Cumberland County. Many iron bridges replaced former wooden bridges. Cumberland County was originally part of Lancaster County until it became a separate county on January 27, 1750.

This metal deck girder railroad bridge was built by the Pennsylvania Railroad near the village of Peach Bottom in southern Lancaster County. At one time, the original town of Peach Bottom was located across the Susquehanna River in York County. Note the large number of ladies in white dresses on the deck of the bridge who might have been gathered for a wedding.

This elevated York and Hanover trolley bridge was located in Hanover in southwestern York County. The York and Hanover Trolley Line carried passengers from 1908 until 1939. At that time, the trolley business dropped off, and the land was sold to Metropolitan Edison Company for the purpose of constructing transmission lines.

95

This photograph was taken about 1908 at East Troy in western Bradford County. The metal truss bridge in the photograph is not as unusual as the two boys clinging to the ends of the bridge. How did they get up there, and, better yet, how are they going to get down?

The Spruce Street Bridge is a through truss metal bridge built in Scranton in central Lackawanna County. Lackawanna County is the youngest of Pennsylvania's 67 counties, having been formed in 1878. *Lackawanna* is an old Native American word meaning "where the streams meet."

This Williamsport metal truss bridge was over the Loyalsock Creek at Williamsport in south-central Lycoming County. At first glance, this appears to be one bridge. Upon a closer look, there are really two bridges here. The trolley bridge is a separate bridge from the roadway bridge.

This is a six-span metal deck girder railroad bridge at Martins Creek in Northampton County. This bridge was built by the Northampton Railroad that later became part of the Lehigh and New England Railway. Note that there is a man walking on the bridge.

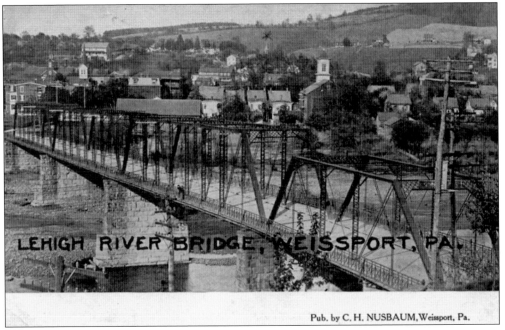

Pub. by C. H. NUSBAUM, Weissport, Pa.

This 1890 metal truss bridge replaced a covered bridge between Lehighton and Weissport in Carbon County. This photograph shows the four-span iron bridge crossing over the Lehigh River with the town of Weissport in the background. Weissport was named after Col. Jacob Weiss, who organized an early coal company. Weissport served as the only canal boat building and repair yard along the Lehigh Canal.

The bridge above is the Hamilton Street Bridge in Allentown. A trolley is shown passing over the bridge, and in the foreground is part of a canal lock belonging to the Lehigh Canal. Allentown is the third-most populated city in Pennsylvania behind Philadelphia and Pittsburgh.

Easton, Pa. Road Bridge.

This early postcard of a metal truss bridge over the Lehigh River and canal at Easton in Northampton County shows a trolley, a horse and wagon, and a pedestrian all crossing the bridge. In the background appears to be a bridge that crosses over top of this bridge.

Looking up Lehigh River & Canal, Easton, Pa.

This postcard view from another angle shows a metal truss train bridge crossing over top of the metal truss vehicular bridge at Easton. The presence of railroad tracks on both banks of the river serves to remind people of how important railroads once were.

5600—View of Reading from Penn St. Bridge, Reading. Pa.

The Penn Street Bridge was a double-intersecting Pratt truss built by Berks County in 1885 over the Schuylkill River in Reading. In the background is the city of Reading, and in the foreground are the banks of West Reading. The large building to the left of the bridge on the Reading side is the Pennsylvania Railroad passenger station.

READING, FROM THE BRIDGE, READING, PA.

The Zeno Chewing Gum Company used postcards to advertise its gum. In this photograph, which is the same as the previous one, Zeno superimposed a barn over top of the train freight station to the right of the bridge. The barn served as a way to insert its slogan "Zeno Means Good Chewing Gum." If postcards give a message, the message this postcard gives is "don't always believe what is seen."

THE S BRIDGE OVER THE SCHUYLKILL
RIVER AT MANAYUNK, PHILADELPHIA, PA.

The S Bridge over Schuylkill River at Manayunk was built in 1884 by the Pennsylvania Railroad. The unusual S-shaped bridge was well known in the area because of its shape. By 1917, the bridge became weak and was replaced with a Spanish arched concrete bridge. Manayunk got its name from the Lenape Indians, and loosely translated, it means "our place for drinking."

This is a 1909 postcard of the Strawberry Hill Bridge at Strawberry Mansion, a part of Fairmount Park in northern Philadelphia. This steel bridge was built in 1897 over the Schuylkill River and has a length of 1,250 feet. Strawberry Mansion was named after a large mansion that, for a short period of time, was a restaurant that was famous for its strawberries and cream.

This River Drive Bridge was built over the Schuylkill River and River Drive in the Fairmount Park section of Philadelphia. This railroad bridge was a combination of stone arch and metal with the main section over the river being a metal truss deck bridge. Fairmount Park is one of the largest municipal public parks in the world and was the site of the 1876 Philadelphia Centennial Exposition.

Philadelphia. Girard Ave. Bridge, Fairmount Park.

The Girard Avenue Bridge was built during 1873 and 1874 over the Schuylkill River in Philadelphia. The bridge was built for the 1876 Philadelphia centennial as an entrance to the zoological gardens, which can be seen in the foreground. The bridge was 100 feet wide, the widest iron truss built to date at that time.

TEN DOLLARS FINE FOR DRIVING OVER THIS BRIDGE FASTER THAN A WALK.

BRIDGE OVER THE DELAWARE RIVER, LEADING TO MATAMORAS, MILFORD AND DINGMAN'S FERRY, PENN., PORT JERVIS, N. Y.

A fine for crossing or driving over a bridge faster than a walk was found on quite a few of the earlier and longer wooden bridges and iron bridges. This Pennsylvania–Petit truss bridge crossed the Delaware River in northern Pike County. Pike County is named for Zebulon Pike, an explorer who mapped much of the southern portion of the Louisiana Purchase.

This is the 1896 Northampton Street Bridge over the Delaware River between Easton, Pennsylvania, and Phillipsburg, New Jersey. The bridge is often mistaken for a suspension bridge because of its shape. This bridge was designed by James Madison Porter and replaced Timothy Palmer's 1806 covered bridge, and it is listed as a national civil engineering landmark. This photograph was taken from the Phillipsburg side of the river looking toward Easton.

This is a photograph of the Old McConkey's Ferry Inn and the metal bridge at Washington Crossing. The iron bridge replaced a covered bridge at this location that had six spans and was 875 feet long. During the Revolutionary War, the inn served as a meeting place for Gen. George Washington and his officers before he and his army crossed the Delaware River in boats on Christmas night in 1776. They attacked Hessian troops camped at Trenton, New Jersey, and it was this victory that changed the tide of the war.

The Tacony-Palmyra Bridge was built over the Delaware River during 1928 and 1929. The eight-span bridge supports four lanes of traffic and connects Philadelphia to Palmyra, New Jersey. The 3,658-foot-long bridge was designed by Ralph Modjeski and replaced the Tacony-Palmyra Ferry at this location.

New Bridge over Susquehanna River, Sayre, Pa.

Handcolored.

The Sayre Bridge was located over the Susquehanna River at Sayre in northern Bradford County, about a mile and a half south of the New York state line. The bridge was a three-span Pennsylvania Pratt truss. The Susquehanna River is over 400 miles long and starts in Otsego Lake in New York, flows through Pennsylvania, and empties into the Chesapeake Bay.

This postcard depicts the new iron girder railroad bridge and the older iron Baltimore Pratt truss railroad bridge that it replaced. Because the Baltimore and Ohio Railroad developed this subtype of Pratt truss, the truss type took the name of the Baltimore and Ohio Railroad. The truss became widely used by various railroads in their bridge construction. The two Lehigh Valley railroad bridges on the postcard crossed the North Branch of the Susquehanna River at Towanda. The postmark on this postcard is July 16, 1907.

This is a four-span Baltimore truss railroad bridge over the Susquehanna River at Standing Stone in central Bradford County. Standing Stone was named after a Native American village at this location by the same name.

This Berwick–Nescopeck Bridge replaced a covered bridge at this location that was destroyed by a flood in 1904. In 1906, the York Bridge Company built this iron truss bridge between Berwick in Columbia County and Nescopeck in Luzerne County at a cost of $209,500.

This is a side view of the Berwick–Nescopeck Bridge across the Susquehanna River. This Pennsylvania Pratt truss iron bridge was replaced during 1980 and 1981. *Nescopeck* is an Algonquian word meaning "black spring."

NEW BRIDGE. DANVILLE, PA.   7190

The Danville Bridge over the Susquehanna River is another example of a Pennsylvania Pratt truss bridge. Note the trolley stopped on the bridge. The men are on the left side of the bridge, and the ladies are on the right side of the bridge. In the early 1900s, it was customary for the men to stand together and for the ladies to stand together. When they would get on the trolley, the women went first and sat together, and then the men followed. Times have changed.

1— View from Blue Hill
North and West Branches of Susquehanna River
at Northumberland and Sunbury, Pa.

At Northumberland the West and North Branches of the Susquehanna River join together. The 1927 concrete bridge in the foreground was once a covered bridge. On the right, the upper metal vehicular bridge and the lower metal railroad bridge were also at one time covered bridges connecting Northumberland to Sunbury.

This was the new Lewisburg iron truss roadway bridge over the West Branch of the Susquehanna River. Prior to the building of this bridge, roadway traffic as well as the railroad shared the covered bridge that can be seen on the extreme left of the photograph. Lewisburg was named after Ludwig (Lewis) Doerr, an early settler in this area.

This is an end view of the Northumberland Railroad bridge connecting the town of Northumberland to Union County over the West Branch of the Susquehanna River. Just south of here the North and West Branches of the Susquehanna River join together.

This was the Pennsylvania and Reading Railroad bridge over the Susquehanna River at Sunbury. The small rectangle sign at the entrance of the bridge prohibits pedestrians from walking over the bridge. The sign states, "Notice, All Persons Are Forbidden to Cross This Bridge." The message on the back of this postcard reads, "Having a dandy time, going to the circus Wednesday. Regards to Mrs. B. Don't sew any more button holes up while I am gone." The postcard is postmarked May 28, 1907.

This 1908 Sunbury tollhouse was at the entrance to the Sunbury-Shamokin Dam Bridge. Tolls were collected on the right side of the building while a store with small travel items was on the left. The toll collector lived on the second floor. It has been said that there was a beautiful view up and down the river from the second floor.

New Bridge, crossing Susquehanna River, Sunbury, Pa.

216871

This is a better view of the Sunbury–Shamokin Dam Bridge taken from the Sunbury side of the Susquehanna River. A trolley can be seen traveling over the bridge. The town of Shamokin Dam is named after an early dam that was in the Susquehanna River between the east and west shore of the river. Before the iron bridge was built, the dam provided water deep enough for a ferry crossing at this location. The dam was destroyed in 1904 by an ice jam.

The People's Bridge, also known as the Walnut Street Bridge, spans the Susquehanna River at Harrisburg. The bridge consists of 14 Baltimore trusses and was built in 1890 by the Phoenix Bridge Company. The bridge was built as a free bridge in order to break the tolls charged by the nearby Camelback Bridge (Market Street Bridge). In 1972, the 2,801-foot-long bridge was weakened by a flood. It has since been closed to roadway traffic and is open only to pedestrian traffic.

Entrance to Market St. Bridge, Harrisburg, Pa.

Note the tall thin columns at the entrance to the 1902 Market Street Bridge in Harrisburg. These red sandstone columns are from the old state capitol building that burned in 1879. This postcard shows the bridge between 1902 and 1927 when it was still a two-lane metal girder bridge.

Cumberland Valley Bridge crossing the Susquehanna river   Harrisburg, Pa.

This is the second Cumberland Valley Railroad bridge at Harrisburg. The first bridge at this site was a wooden bridge where trains used the flat roof for crossing the Susquehanna River while cars traveled in two lanes inside the enclosed covered part of the bridge.

The Columbia-Wrightsville Bridge was a railroad bridge built by the Pennsylvania Railroad in 1896. The one-track railroad bridge was also used as a two-lane vehicular bridge. Cars had to wait their turn when trains were using the bridge. Originally it was meant to have two levels—one for the railroad and one for vehicular traffic; however, that never materialized.

The Columbia-Wrightsville Bridge, with a length of 5,375 feet, was the longest metal bridge in the world. The bridge was built over the Susquehanna River in just 21 days. The bridge was dismantled in the early 1960s.

"Peep" through 5,375 feet of the P. R. R. Bridge. Wrightsville, P
he Star, Publishers.

As one looks through the Columbia-Wrightsville Bridge over the Susquehanna River, the opening at the other end of the bridge that is over a mile away can barely be seen. This was the longest metal bridge in the world. The sign on the left of the bridge proclaims a 10-mile-per-hour speed limit over the bridge (unless one is being chased by a train).

Six

CONCRETE BRIDGES

CLARION RIVER BRIDGE, RIDGWAY, PA.

When most people think of an arch truss bridge with uprights they think of a wooden bridge. But this unusual bowstring arch truss bridge was made of concrete. The Ridgway Bridge was built in the early 1900s over the Clarion River at Ridgway in Elk County. Note the fancy five-globe lights on the poles at the four corners of the bridge. Today the bridge no longer exists, but the town of Ridgway has maintained many of its original Victorian homes that were built in the late 1800s.

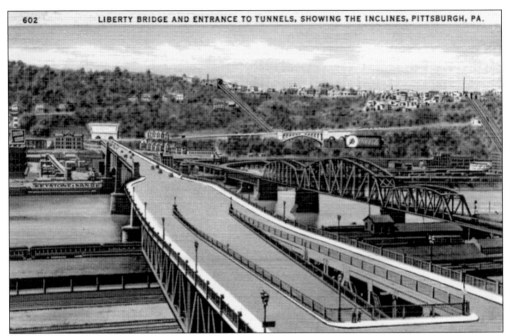

Pittsburgh's Liberty Bridge leads from downtown Pittsburgh into twin tunnels. The bridge was built in 1927 at a cost of $3.5 million and is the longest bridge in the city limits with a length of 2,662 feet. Note the other two bridges in background. Over 700 bridges are located within the city limits of Pittsburgh. Only the city of Venice, Italy, has more bridges.

PA-608   *George Westinghouse Memorial Bridge and Plants on Lincoln Highway*

The George Westinghouse Memorial Bridge is located 12 miles east of Pittsburgh on Route 30. At the time of its completion in 1932, the bridge was the highest open-spandrel concrete arch bridge (at 240 feet off the valley floor) in the United States. The large Westinghouse plant, known for its brand of electrical products and after which the bridge was named, can be seen below the bridge. This is a linen-era postcard.

Mulberry Street Bridge, largest Concrete Bridge in the World, Harrisburg, Pa.

The Mulberry Street Viaduct in Harrisburg, with a length of 1,600 feet, was the largest concrete bridge in the world at its time of completion in 1909. The bridge, with its unusual sharp turn in the roadway, crosses Cameron Street, South Tenth Street, Paxton Creek, and the Norfolk Southern and Amtrak railway yards. Note the unusual metal pipe railing along the sides of the bridge.

The Soldiers and Sailors Memorial Bridge serves as an eastern approach to the capitol complex in Harrisburg. What makes this bridge unusual are the large 300-foot-high memorial pylons at the approach to the bridge built as a memorial to those who fought in World War I. Also of interest are the arch keystones that have the shape of different military objects. The $4 million bridge was dedicated in 1930 and carries State Street from Allison Hill to Fisher Plaza. This is a linen-era postcard.

The Nicholson Viaduct was built by the Delaware, Lackawanna and Western Railroad near Scranton in Wyoming County. In this 1915 photograph, one of the center arches still has construction work being done on the bridge. The bridge was locally referred to as the ninth wonder of the world because of its size.

With a height of 240 feet above the stream level, the Nicholson Viaduct, at the time of its construction in 1915, was the considered the highest concrete arch railroad bridge in the world. The bridge spans the Tunkhannock Creek and a valley and has a total length of 2,375 feet. The bridge is still in use today.

Two trolleys or streetcars can be seen on this postcard of the Eighth Street Bridge in Allentown. The 2,650-foot-long bridge was built by the Lehigh Valley Transit Company in 1913 as a streetcar and interurban line bridge connecting Allentown and South Allentown. This postcard is an interesting study in geometric shapes. Notice how the arches get smaller as they fade into the distance.

This concrete bridge over the Lehigh River between Bethlehem and South Bethlehem is referred to as the Hill to Hill Bridge. The bridge was built in 1924 at a cost of $2,368,000. The four-lane bridge has a total length of 6,500 feet and has a sharp turn near the center of the bridge. The city of Bethlehem was founded in 1741 and is nicknamed "Christmas City USA."

nov 29 1947

SCHUYLKILL AVENUE BRIDGE, SPANNING THE SCHUYLKILL RIVER, READING, PA.
Completed in 1925, of reinforced concrete at a cost of $639,650.46. Replacing Open Iron Deck structure erected in 1893. First bridge at this site, known as "Kissinger's Covered Bridge", erected in 1810.

The Schuylkill Avenue Bridge was built in 1925 and is one of three bridges across the Schuylkill River entering the city of Reading from the west. This concrete arch bridge replaced a former iron bridge that had become deteriorated from the smoke and cinders of the trains that traveled beneath the iron bridge. The iron bridge replaced a former covered bridge at this location.

BINGAMAN STREET BRIDGE, READING, PA.

The Bingaman Street Bridge was built in 1921 over the Schuylkill River in Reading to eliminate the grade crossing at the eastern end of the old iron bridge at Bingaman and Third Streets. This was accomplished by having a longer approach to the concrete bridge. The iron bridge replaced the former 585–foot–long covered bridge. Note the bend in the bridge on the West Reading side of the river.

THE PENN STREET VIADUCT CROSSING THE SCHUYLKILL RIVER, READING, PA.

Work started Oct. 16, 1911. Dedicated May 23, 1914. Length 1350 feet. Width 80 feet. Total weight of material used, 111,505,448 pounds. Total cost of erection $568,675.28. First covered bridge erected 1815. Destroyed by flood, Sept. 1841. Second bridge erected 1851. Third, an iron bridge, 1884.

The Penn Street Viaduct was opened to traffic on Friday, November 12, 1913, at 5:14 p.m. The concrete bridge crosses the Schuylkill River and is the main bridge leading into the city of Reading. The bridge was built at a cost of $568,675.28 and replaced an earlier through iron truss bridge, which had replaced a 600-foot-long covered bridge that was built in 1815 at a cost of $49,297.

PENN STREET BRIDGE, READING, PA.

This linen-era postcard shows the Penn Street Viaduct and the city of Reading from the West Reading side of the river. The bridge has 26 concrete columns and originally had four globe lights on each column. In this photograph taken during the 1940s, the four-globe lights on the columns have been replaced with one light.

During the time of its construction in 1927, this bridge in Reading was referred to as the Mineral Spring Viaduct. Charles A. Lindbergh made the first transatlantic flight in the same year. The flight of Lindbergh was so impressive that the name of the bridge during its construction was changed to the Lindbergh Viaduct. Incidentally Lindbergh's flight from New York to Paris took 33.5 hours to fly. The postcard is from the linen era.

R104　LINDBERGH VIADUCT, SHOWING PAGODA, READING, PA.　2505-30

The Lindbergh Viaduct, with its long arches and a serpentine-shaped roadway, is perhaps the most graceful of all the Reading bridges. The bridge is the only bridge on the eastern side of Reading leading into the city.

9. WALNUT LANE BRIDGE OVER WISSAHICKON, LARGEST CONCRETE BRIDGE EVER BUILT, PHILADELPHIA, PA

The Walnut Lane Bridge was built over the Wissahickon Creek near a part of Philadelphia called Germantown. At the time of its construction in 1906, the main arch of this bridge was the world's longest concrete arch, measuring 233 feet across. Over 40,000 tons of concrete were used to build all five arches of the bridge. The cost of the bridge exceeded $260,000.

Philadelphia - Walnut Lane Bridge.

This is a rare postcard view of the construction of the Walnut Lane Bridge. Note all the wooden framework and scaffolding that had to be built in the construction of this bridge. Steel reinforcing rods were then inserted in this framework and concrete was poured. When this framework was being removed, part of it collapsed, sending several workers nearly 200 feet into the creek. One man was killed and several others were seriously injured.

The nearby Henry Avenue Bridge was similar in design and was also built across the Wissahickon Creek in Philadelphia. This graceful arch bridge was completed in 1932 and was designed by Ralph Modjeski. The bridge is 192 feet above the water level of the creek. Modjeski joined forces with Frank Masters, and together they designed many other architecturally significant bridges, including the Market Street Bridge in Harrisburg, the Clarks Ferry Bridge, and three Philadelphia bridges, the Ben Franklin Bridge, the Tacony-Palmyra Bridge, and the Walt Whitman Bridge.

This is the new concrete Pennsylvania Railroad bridge over the Schuylkill River and River Drive in Fairmount Park in Philadelphia. This bridge replaced a combination stone and iron bridge at this location. Note that River Drive goes through a tunnel. Fairmount Park covers nearly 2,000 acres of land.

The Market Street Bridge in Wilkes-Barre was built between 1926 and 1929 over the North Branch of the Susquehanna River at Wilkes-Barre. This bridge is one of the most highly ornamental reinforced concrete bridges in Pennsylvania. The 12-arch bridge has two pylons at each approach, on top of which are large carved limestone eagles. Fancy balustrades line the edges of the bridge. The bridge also originally had an operable water-gauging station on the bridge.

This reinforced concrete bridge was built in 1927 over the West Branch of the Susquehanna River between Northumberland and Union County. The bridge carried Route 11 over the Susquehanna River. In the early part of the 20th century, this road was part of the Susquehanna Trail, an informal automobile route that ran from Washington, D.C., to Niagara Falls, New York. In the early days of the automobile, there were many of these trails, usually marked by colored bands painted on telephone poles that helped direct travelers.

Clarks Ferry Bridge was built during the years 1923 to 1925 between Perry and Dauphin Counties at Duncannon. The bridge was built by Ralph Modjeski and Frank Masters at a cost of $700,000. It carries Route 22 and Route 322 and the Appalachian Trail over the Susquehanna River. The Appalachian Trail, a unit of the National Park Service, is 2,175 miles long and runs from Katahdin, Maine, to Springer Mountain, Georgia. This postcard is postmarked March 29, 1929.

This is the 1928 four-lane Market Street Bridge over the Susquehanna River at Harrisburg. This bridge was also designed by Modjeski and Masters and was the third bridge at this location. The original bridge was Theodore Burr's Camelback Bridge, followed in 1902 by a steel girder bridge. The Susquehanna River has been referred to by geologists as the oldest or the second-oldest major waterway in the world.

The Cumberland Valley Railroad bridge was the third railroad bridge at this location. The original bridge was a Town truss double-deck wooden bridge built in 1836. Inside the lower level was a two-lane roadway, and the roof was for the railroad. In 1856, an iron bridge replaced the wooden bridge, and in 1916, this concrete arch bridge was built.

lumbia-Wrightsville Bridge
n York, Pa. and Columbia, Pa.
argest Bridge Spanning the
Susquehanna River

umbia-Wrightsville Bridge over the Susquehanna River, at the time of its construction)29 to 1930, was considered the longest concrete arch bridge in the world. The bridge has and has a total length of 7,374 feet (American Society of Civil Engineers measurement). ge is listed on the National Register of Historic Places and is also considered a historic ,ineering landmark. This concrete bridge replaced the longest iron truss bridge in the which in turn replaced the longest covered bridge in the world.

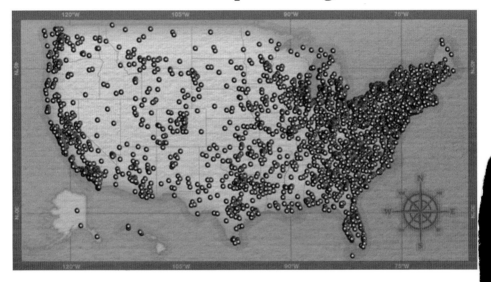